Hashgraph
VS
Blockchain

#*THE FUTURE OF*
CRYPTOCURRENCY

Mario Robertson

© 2018

Please note the information contained in this document is for educational and entertainment purposes only. Every attempt has been made to provide accurate, up to date and reliable, complete information. No warranties of any kind are expressed or implied. Readers acknowledge that the author is not engaging in the rendering of legal, financial, medical or professional advice. The content of this book has been derived from various sources. Please consult a licensed professional before attempting any techniques outlined in this book.

By reading this document, the reader agrees that under no circumstances is the author responsible for any losses, direct or indirect, which are incurred as a result of the use of information contained within this document, including, but not limited to, —errors, omissions, or inaccuracies.

INTRODUCTION: #BIG CHANGES ARE ALREADY IN MOTION

Our current capitalist system is in the midst of a big change, a change that is likely to be made by the continued advancement of technology.

CAPITALISM IS *GETTING* OLD

Let's face it, our current capitalist society is starting to look pretty dated and unless the world randomly decides to shake-up and modernize how finance and banking function, it looks like in the next 20 to 30 years we may be living in a very unequal world. Experiments in different forms of capitalist democracy have had varying degrees of success, but in the end, the older elements of the system always bring it down.

Many feel though that capitalism cannot be replaced, that it is a normal part of human nature. There is some truth in this, but the world has not always been the same and, most importantly, the world's problems have not always been the same either. This is especially true when considering the deteriorating state of the environment, global warming and also the ever-inflating world population, currently at 7.6 billion.

Often people who strongly defend capitalism will point to the collapse of communism, the ultimate critic of capitalism. Though it is true that communist regimes failed to provide a viable alternative to capitalism, as a social experiment, it showed us that there are options that can be explored through policy, regulation and production. It is not that capitalism needs to be completely dismantled, but it needs to evolve into a new structure that reflects the world we are now living in.

Of course, when we speak of capitalism, we should remember that it has existed for a long time in different forms, constantly evolving from one form to another. The capitalist world outlined by Karl Marx in *Das Kapital* is not the same as the world we live in today, though some of his observations still persevere. The current form of capitalism we use is sometimes referred to as 'neoliberal capitalism' and it is employed around much of the world. With this form of capitalism, what we are seeing is governments have less influence and are shrinking in size, equality is growing and more and more wealth is swallowed up by many of the richest individuals and corporations. This has contributed to a slowing down of economic growth worldwide in the last few years. When large amounts of wealth are consumed by the super-rich, much of that money usually goes unspent and when that happens there is less money for an economy to continue working.

If we don't make changes, we may end up living in a world where most of the wealth has been devoured by the elite 1% while the rest of us struggle just to get by - where economies are increasingly unstable and economic crashes are a far too often occurrence - where wages fail to rise alongside inflation, where taxes fail to fund governments and where the public and private world are both enslaved by debt.

But neoliberal capitalism is not the whole issue. In fact, it emerged largely in the 1980s as an alternative to the form of capitalism that preceded it, which was based on the ideas of John Maynard Keynes, and inherited many of its problems. Many of these problems can be traced back all the way to the Industrial

Revolution of the 1800s, with a little bit of reshaping here and there, mostly in the form of policymaking and technology. Perhaps the biggest of all those problems is that capitalism needs constant growth. Economic stagnation kills it. To fuel that growth, money needs to come from somewhere, and often in our times, this is from cutting governmental services and relaxing financial regulation. It is an issue that may never be fixed but it has led to the situation we are in now.

The death of the current capitalist system is something that's being discussed a lot by industry leaders and economists, with many looking for new ways to revitalize or reshape it. One of the most vocal individuals is economist Joseph Stiglitz, who has even gone as far as saying neoliberal capitalism was already dead back in 2016. He believes that the euphoria that once surrounded neoliberalism in the 1980s has now faded, arguing that the basis of neoliberalism - that markets work best when there is no regulation, without government involvement - has been disproven, both in terms of policy and academically.

But it's not just experts who feel this way. A distrust of the current capitalist system has been growing for some time now, largely triggered by the events that followed the 2008 financial crash. People have lost a lot of trust in banking and large corporations. In fact, in 2014, it was reported by Time that 71% of millennials would rather go to a dentist to get teeth removed than listen to a bank's message. The EU can also see similar trends in the lack of young people's interest in Internet banking in a 2016 survey. On top of that, statistics released by The Washington Post in 2016 show that more than half (51%) of millennials from the US now reject capitalism. What makes it more worrying is that we have an aging world population, an issue that is fast approaching. Unless trust is restored in the young, these institutions have no future. It doesn't matter what side of the political spectrum you are on or how versed you are in economics, we all know that unless something changes, trouble lies ahead.

Neoliberal capitalism has faced some enormous challenges over the past few years and it has not handled them all that well. Largely, this is down to its slow and often inadequate response to change. Instead, it clings on to traditional ideas of what capitalism should be, ideas that worked perhaps 30-40 years ago, in a different economic environment. One such change, which actually evolved out of neoliberal capitalism, is globalization. Globalization is perhaps one of the biggest developments of the late 20th century and early 21st. It took shape from a mixture of both technological change and political change, both driven by capitalism.

At first globalization was hailed as a great achievement, bringing the world closer together. But over time it became clear that many people felt left out from this development and in fact felt the opposite was true, that their lives were getting worse. As a result of this, we are seeing the world close off from itself.

Far-right groups, taking advantage of this discontent, are now more powerful than they used to be and are influencing politics with their reactionary views on issues such as immigration. Such political stances have a negative impact on how people work together across the world. The UK leaving the EU is a prime example of this, as is the presidency of

Donald Trump in the USA. In order to prevent further divisions in our globalized world, we need to put something in place that can help keep it together.

We've almost come to a deadlock where we're unable to see a different future where money is distributed more equally among the young and the poor, men and women, the developed first world nations and the lesser developed third world. Politicians in most parts of the world don't seem to have a clue how to fix any of these problems any more - they are no longer the innovators of change and policy they once were. This is also partly as a result of neoliberal capitalism eroding their power by shrinking their institutions.

A new form of capitalism is needed to help save the world and keep mankind progressing or we may elapse into a less stable world. It must remove the shackles of the old problems our current capitalist system has. This new form of capitalism needs to fit in with the emerging data-driven economy, which is slowly, but surely taking over. The new world may not necessarily be a perfect one, but it's a change that is looking like it's desperately needed.

TECHNOLOGY IS THE DRIVING-FORCE

OF CHANGE

But change hasn't completely grinded to a halt, positive things are still happening daily. You just need to know where to look for them. Technology in the 21st century has boomed on so many levels making many work-related tasks easier. In some senses, it is one of the only real ways the world is still improving.

Technological change also has a strong long-lasting friendship with capitalism. In fact, if it was not for the invention of the steam pump, we would never have had the industrial revolution, which kick-started what we now call capitalism. Almost all of the biggest inventions have had some effect on capitalism and sometimes end up changing how it works. The Internet is one of the best and most recent examples of this. It has completely changed how people do business.

One of the biggest changes that is still in motion is the implementation of AI in the workplace. We are now increasingly relying on AI to fulfill tasks that were previously handled by human beings. The number of areas it can be applied to is unreal - from business, administration, customer services, healthcare, education, data collection - the list doesn't stop growing. There are even AI-based law advisers now. Though this has huge benefits for industry, it is very possible that we may see an epidemic of mass unemployment, which could have huge political consequences. Or we may see a miracle take place where more and more individuals retrain in IT and the world's economy becomes a place almost 100% data-orientated. In such a world, we may see people being freed from their mundane past jobs and being able to follow their true passions if some kind of compensation is put in place, such as a universal basic income. AI has both positive and negative side effects depending on how responsibly society acts to those changes. Either way, it will lead to change and we are yet to see the full scope of it.

Some will thrive, some will fail and some will disappear. Whatever position you find yourself in, you know that in the 21st century it was most likely technology that got you there. The risk is there, but with all change there is a risk, and changes never fully benefit everyone.

WHAT DOES THAT CHANGE LOOK LIKE?

However the world responds to these changes it's clear that technology is the driving force behind the new world we are rapidly heading toward. We all need to recognize this. One of those changes is how we deal with money. In this ebook, we will discuss how the world of finance is in the process of being rocked off its feet. No matter how much they try to pretend everything is fine, we know it's not and big changes are in the process of happening right now. These changes are going to clear out all the old banking and finance cronies and create a new system. It all started with the creation of blockchain and are gaining ground day by day. It scares the hell out of the banking world elites and politicians because it will remove their control over how transactions will be made and will make current regulations obsolete.

But the genius invention of blockchain isn't the final solution to the world's financial issues, it's just the platform where the next invention has sprung out of - **Hashgraph**. In the following chapters, we will map how we got to this point, explaining how it all works, the benefits Hashgraph has to offer the world, and why it should host the next big cryptocurrency and become the future of how we all handle transactions. Disregard Bitcoin, Ethereum and other blockchain-based technology, Hashgraph is the true contender.

TABLE OF CONTENTS

CHAPTER 1: #BLOCKCHAIN, WHERE IT ALL BEGAN

Blockchain is the technology most cryptocurrencies are built upon, including Bitcoin. Without it, cryptocurrency would not exist.

WHAT IS BLOCKCHAIN? (IN SIMPLE TERMS)

Explained in the simplest of terms, blockchain is basically a decentralized database of records where information can be shared between one another directly without having to pass through a third-party. Because it is decentralized, no specific individual can control it leading many to believe it is the most democratic way to share information or in this make transactions. Most of the information stored on a blockchain consists of who owns what. It also is constantly being updated on a distributed ledger, which is visible to everyone on it. Still not sure you get it? Then continue reading - all will be explained.

The first ever blockchain was created by a mysterious person or group named Satoshi Nakamoto for their cryptocurrency, Bitcoin, in around 2008 (coincidentally the same year as one of the largest financial crashes). Very little is known about Satoshi as they mysteriously disappeared very soon after Bitcoin started to gain momentum. However, that didn't stop the Bitcoin/blockchain community from continuing to work on it (see the next chapter, *Chapter 2: #The Emergence of Bitcoin*).

Blockchain has a huge potential. Some truly see it as the evolution of the world's economy. It may even be able to fix the problem with globalization by providing a network where everyone on the planet can do business and pay for services without extortionate fees. On top of that, it may well be an even playing field where issues of inequality are removed. For bankers, the fact that blockchain is 'decentralized' is terrifying. One of the many ways banks make money is by being the middlemen in between transactions and they know that if all currency suddenly became part of a blockchain, or blockchains, they will have absolutely no power.

Since those early days, blockchain technology has been used to build numerous other crypto-currencies such as Ethereum, Litecoin, Dogecoin, Steem… the list goes on.

HOW DOES IT WORK?

The way blockchain works may seem a little confusing at first, but once you understand the principles, it is very logical.

When a transaction of cryptocurrency takes place on blockchain, it needs to be selected by a 'miner' who adds it into a newly created 'block' along with a number of other transactions. Usually miners select which transactions they will include in the new block by whichever has the best mining fee for completing the transaction. This often means that individuals willing to pay more to miners have their transactions completed faster than those who pay less. Despite this, miners are only able to add a limited amount of transactions to their block. This is seen as fair, because it rules out the benefit of having a more powerful computer, which may be able to handle potentially larger blocks with larger rewards and fees.

Once this transaction is added to the block, it will contain all the information about the transaction that took place, such as who it was between, the date and time of the transaction, where it took place, and information of other recent transactions that happened around the same time. Once all the transactions have been added to the block, the miner can start mining (or decrypting if you will) all the information. This usually means solving immensely complicated mathematical equations. It should be mentioned that 'mining' is a huge task and often requires very powerful computers (often computers designed for gamers are the best for this), and a lot of time - often more than a day for just one block. Some companies in places such as China existed purely to mine cryptocurrencies, such as Bitcoin.

Miners also need to validate their blocks, which involves checking for any fraudulent transactions. If there are any fraudulent transactions within the block, the blockchain will not accept it, which may result in the miner losing a large part of a chain they have created if they are not careful. By mining and validating, miners are keeping the system safe, but validating a block can also be a very time-consuming part of the process. Once the mining process is complete, the block joins the rest of the blockchain (this is where the name 'blockchain' comes from), the all the transactions are complete and fully processed, and the miner gains the mining fees from the individuals who created the initial transactions and is rewarded with newly cryptocurrency for creating a new block by the system. This is also the number one way new cryptocurrency is distributed - the more people there are out their mining blocks, the more of a cryptocurrency is distributed among the network. However, it should be mentioned that some cryptocurrencies, such as Bitcoin, were designed to limit the amount of cryptocurrency that can be created.

One of the most interesting things about blockchain is that all blocks and transactions are logged and stored in a ledger. This is done by what is called gossiping, which is where information is shared among computers (often referred to as nodes). This ledger is completely public and can be accessed by anyone, which means no transactions can be hidden. This is an incredibly important part of working on blockchain and many have polarized views on it. Naturally, some feel uncomfortable with sharing all their transactions with the public, while others hold the opinion that it is a necessary function of blockchain that helps fight fraudulent transactions, such as double-spending. It is also something that concerns many banks and governments. If all suddenly used a blockchain-based cryptocurrency, corrupt officials would not want any illegal transactions to be recorded.

It should also be mentioned that blockchains can operate on different types on algorithms, such as leader-based (sometimes referred to as centralized), which is where all transactions are sent through the leader to be validated and the information is redistributed to the rest of the network, and there is Proof of Work and Proof of Stake - the two most used algorithms - which are explained in the next chapter. There are a few others, but the most important is the voting algorithm, which Hashgraph uses, also discussed more later in the same chapter mentioned above.

A NEW KIND OF INFORMATION

SHARING PLATFORM

Blockchain also has other benefits aside from managing financial transactions. It is a platform where applications can be built on top and is ideal for any kind of data storage. This is mainly down to the fact that it is almost impossible to rewrite or manipulate the data of a block in a blockchain. Industry leaders from all walks of life have considered the uses of blockchain technology, including top medical professionals who see its potential to share medical records for example.

BLOCKCHAINS CAN ALSO BE USED FOR:

- Internal procedures in companies. For example, sharing information among employees.
- Safely sharing or selling intellectual property.

- Safely sharing or selling deeds to physical property, such as homes.
- Setting up contracts between companies and individuals, such as 'Smart Contracts', a feature Ethereum is well known for (discussed further in the next chapter, *Chapter 2: #The Emergence of Bitcoin and Other Cryptocurrencies*).
- Voting - some have explored the possibility of blockchains being used in elections. This is largely because it becomes almost impossible to corrupt as all votes can be logged and viewed in the ledger.

CHAPTER 2: #PROOF OF WORK AND PROOF OF STAKE

Proof of Work (PoW) refers to a specific kind of protocol where the main goal is to prevent cyber-attacks such as DDoS or distributed denial of service. The main purpose for which DDoS attacks are launched by malicious elements of the online world is to wear out or fatigue a computer system's resources or computing power by overwhelming said system with numerous fake requests.

The concept behind PoW has been around long enough that it's actually older than Bitcoin itself. But the brilliant but still anonymous creator of Bitcoin known by the name Satoshi Nakamoto used this concept to the granddaddy of all cryptocurrencies and, in the process, forever changing the way financial transactions are done online. Moni Naor and Cynthia Dwork first published the Proof of Work concept in 1993 but Ari Juels and Markus Jakobsson only coined the formal term in a document that they published sometime in 1999.

When it comes to decentralized ledgers, there's a system that's of particular importance: a trustless and distributed consensus system. What is it? It's a system where users or participants of a financial transaction system don't have to rely on 3rd party services to ensure efficient and secure transactions. Traditional payment methods such as those used by banks, PayPal and credit card companies function as 3rd parties when you conduct financial transactions using their payment services such as when you buy something using your credit card or through a bank account debiting system. These 3rd parties maintain their own transaction database that contains the history and current balances for all accounts maintained with them. Here's a simple illustration of how this works.

Say Mark paid Sheila $150 via bank fund transfer and both of them maintain accounts with Bank of America. In this transaction, Bank of America - as 3rd party - will debit (decrease) Mark's account by $150 and credit (increase) Sheila's bank account by the same amount. Under this transaction, both parties - Mark and Sheila - implicitly trust Bank of America to do what's right as a 3rd party to their financial transaction.

Blockchain-based transactions - such as Bitcoin and other cryptocurrencies - don't need a 3rd party like Bank of America to validate and execute transactions because, by nature, blockchains distribute all information regarding transactions to all users so that transactions or information on such transactions can be verified directly by any of the users or parties to the transaction. And this is done - as you already know - through the mining process.

So how are mining and the concept of PoW related? Mining, which consists of defined computer calculations required for groups of trustless transactions to be authenticated and created, requires proof of work before being added to the distributed ledger or blockchain. Mining is done for 2 important reasons: secure transactions by verifying transactions' legitimacy and preventing double-spending, and to create new units of a cryptocurrency to entice miners to continue the mining process. To get a better picture of how this works, here are the things that happen when a transaction is set:

- A transaction, along with many others, is grouped together to form a block;
- Miners work to solve complex algorithms to authenticate the legitimacy of every transaction that comprises the block;
- After solving complex algorithms that allow authenticate the transactions, the miners are rewarded with newly minted units of a particular cryptocurrency; and
- The authenticated transactions are added to that particular cryptocurrency's blockchain.

The complex algorithms that miners solve to authenticate transactions have a very important characteristic, which is asymmetry.

Asymmetry in this context is also known by other terms such as CPU pricing function, computational puzzle, client puzzle, or CPU cost function. Asymmetry in terms of what? Asymmetry in terms of difficulty, i.e., these algorithms are relatively easy to check for the network but much harder to do so from the side of the transactions' requesters.

If you recall, all miners of a particular cryptocurrency network have to beat all others to the draw when it comes to solving these complex mathematical problems or algorithms by using nothing but pure computing power in order to make a big enough number of attempts to successfully do so. As the winning miner is able to solve an algorithm, that miner broadcasts it to everyone in the network simultaneously in order to claim his or her reward in accordance with that cryptocurrency's protocol. This is competitive model of authenticating transactions is the essence of the Proof of Work concept.

From a purely technical vantage point, the process of mining for new cryptocurrency units may be considered as inverse hashing, i.e., it determines a nonce or number in order for a specific cryptographic hash algorithm assigned to a specific block of transactions to yield results that don't exceed the threshold. Also referred to as "difficulty" this threshold is responsible for determining the level of competition for mining for a specific cryptocurrency. What this means is that as a network's computing power increases over time, so too do the parameters governing it also rise, which leads to an increasing number of calculations required to authenticate transactions and create new blocks. These parameters change at an average of every 2 weeks or 14 days, which increase mining costs and compel miners to look for ways to improve their operational efficiency to continue being profitable.

It's not only Bitcoin that uses PoW for mining operations but also Ethereum and other altcoins' blockchains. But not all PoW systems are alike. This is because each blockchain has a uniquely created PoW system but in essence, the principle underlying the PoW systems of each cryptocurrency are the same.

PROOF OF STAKE (POS)

The other method for authenticating cryptocurrency transactions and achieving the required distribution consensus is Proof of Stake or PoS for brevity. It's practically the same as PoW in the sense that it still requires solving algorithms to authenticate blocks of transactions but it differs from it in the way it does so. The idea for a PoS framework was first pitched in a 2011 BitcoinTalk forum but it wasn't Bitcoin who first utilized this concept: it was Peercoin back in 2012, followed by Nxt, ShadowCash, NuBits/NuShares, BlackCoin, NavCoin, and Oora.

Compared to the Proof of Work framework of intense competition where miners are able to beat all the others to solve complex equations and are rewarded with new units of a specific cryptocurrency, competition is not intense. In fact, it's not even accurate to think that there's competition among miners under the Proof of Stake framework. Why? It's because miners that work on authenticating blocks of transactions are determined or chosen by the network based on the miners' cryptocurrency shareholdings or overall stake in the cryptocurrency. Hence, there's no intense competition among miners to beat each other to the draw of solving equations and to the corresponding block rewards that come along with being the fastest to solve equations.

Another thing that distinguishes the PoS framework from the PoW system is the incentive or reward. Under the PoS framework, there are no block rewards of newly minted units of a particular cryptocurrency. Why? It's because practically all units of a specific cryptocurrency that utilizes the PoS framework are already minted at the beginning, which makes the number of available units static throughout the process. So what incentive do miners have to authenticate transaction blocks? Transaction fees. And it's for this reason that people who authenticate transactions for blockchains that utilize the PoS framework are called forgers instead of miners.

Why do cryptocurrencies like Ethereum prefer the PoS framework over the PoW one? In particular, why is Ethereum seriously considering transitioning from PoW to PoS?

Under a Proof of Work model, miners use up a lot of energy just to solve an algorithm. Just how much energy? Consider this: It takes the same amount of electricity that roughly 2 American households use daily just to validate one Bitcoin transaction. Yes, the Proof of Work model is that energy-consuming! And electricity consumption of Bitcoin miners only continues to get higher, with a recent study suggesting that by the year 2020, it's possible that Bitcoin miners may consume as much electricity as the nation of Denmark!

And speaking of electricity bills arising from this type of activity, these aren't paid with Bitcoin or other cryptocurrencies but with real ones, e.g., dollars. This may negatively affect the value of cryptocurrencies in the long-term.

As you can see, environmental and economic reasons are 2 of the biggest reasons why the PoS framework is gaining a lot of support.

A new proof of stake consensus protocol is already being tested before implementation by the folks at Ethereum as part of their planned transition from PoW to PoS. This protocol is interestingly named as Casper. Under the Casper protocol, forgers will be selected from a pool of validators, which people can join via application. Ethereum emphasizes that to be included in the validator pool, any user can join at any round they choose regardless of the number of other forger-applicants as there are no parameters or priority schemes for being considered for induction in the validator pool. And once in, the reward for each forger or validator will range from 2% to 15% of the value of the transactions validated, though this isn't a final figure as of now.

Another thing about the Casper protocol is that when officially launched, no limits on the quantity of active validators or forgers will be implemented. Instead, the rewards will be adjusted accordingly when the number of forgers increase or decrease, which is a more natural way of regulating their quantity.

CHAPTER 3: #THE EMERGENCE OF BITCOIN AND OTHER CRYPTOCURRENCIES

Soon after the invention of the blockchain, Bitcoin started to get publicity, some of it pretty critical. Many then started to develop their own cryptocurrency to improve on Bitcoin and overcome its faults.

BITCOIN'S TROUBLED PAST

As mentioned in the previous chapter, Bitcoin was the first cryptocurrency. As with anything challengingly new, it took a while for Bitcoin's popularity to grow and many were unaware of its existence until very recently. On top of that, it also faced immense problems with its image, which prevented it from becoming a trusted alternative from physical currency. This image problem was largely down to Bitcoin being stigmatized as a currency used by the criminal underworld to purchase illegal items such as drugs and weapons. This was done largely on websites such as Silk Road, which was shut down in 2013, and illegal services such as murder for hire, as well as a way to launder money. The media then sensationalized this, which frightened many away from the idea of cryptocurrency, stereotyping all those involved as criminals.

However, as they say: 'all publicity is good publicity'. Despite a damaged reputation, at least people were finally starting to talk about Bitcoin and blockchain technology, and more people started to educate themselves and get involved. We are now even at the point where Bitcoin is such a hot topic for investors its price has skyrocketed in the last few years, almost constantly growing. Further to that, as Bitcoin became more popular with the general public, many criminals that had used the cryptocurrency to carry out their activities have started to abandon it for something less public.

NEW CRYPTOCURRENCIES

Over time people began to see the real benefits Bitcoin had to offer the world and that the image being portrayed was only a small part of the real story. Financial innovators started seeing its potential and leaders working in IT even started using it to pay employees.

However, despite this, some investors and cryptocurrency enthusiasts became tired of Bitcoin for numerous reasons. Some cited issues with the unfocused direction it was going in due to the fact that there were numerous individuals and groups involved in its development and no one was in charge. Such people often cited the issue that unless a direction is decided, Bitcoin may have huge issues with 'scaling' if it ever takes off as a viable alternative to physical currency. 'Scaling' is a term often used in the cryptocurrency community, which refers to how many transactions are able to take place and how much money there is to use. Cryptocurrencies need the infrastructure to cope with handling large amounts of information and generating new money. Bitcoin was never expected to become so widely used and so it was never built to handle so many transactions. In fact, the Bitcoin blockchain was programmed in a specific way to make it harder and harder for new cryptocurrency to be created via mining as time when on, and on top of that, only so much Bitcoin can be made at once, which has made mining Bitcoin incredibly competitive. This is especially true after it gained more popularity from the general public and investors. Further to that, many also started to worry that only 21 million Bitcoins can ever be made. This led many to believe that cryptocurrency may be the future, but perhaps there is a better way, and it was at this point we started to see an explosion of new cryptocurrency.

Perhaps one of the best-known individuals who started working on Bitcoin and left to start their own cryptocurrency is Russian-Canadian Vitalik Buterin, who formerly worked with Bitcoin Magazine. He very quickly went on to develop the platform known as Ethereum, which is perhaps one of Bitcoin's biggest rivals in the cryptocurrency world. Ethereum launched with fantastic success and boasted additional features Bitcoin didn't have, such as 'smart contracts' - a function clients can use to pay those who do tasks for them among a variety of other things. One of the main things people found more promising about Ethereum was that it had a top-down structure. Despite the blockchain itself still operating independently with no third-party interruptions to transactions, Ethereum was being developed directly by the organization that created it, which means it is possible for it to develop and grow with better leadership in comparison to Bitcoin. However, Ethereum also had a number of issues, including the creation of Ethereum Classic (discussed further in *Chapter 5: #Hashgraph vs The Rest of The World*, section *Security… again*).

Despite Bitcoin and Ethereum battling to control the cryptocurrency industry, numerous others also felt the same and developed their own cryptocurrencies, all boasting unique qualities they claim to process. Because of this cryptocurrency explosion, a number of things have happened. Firstly, it raised the profile of

Bitcoin and the idea of cryptocurrency in general, while helping to create a more positive image, an image that appealed to many involved in fintech and other areas of IT.

With a more educated general public, the old image of cryptocurrency began to disappear and slowly but surely governments began to look into its potential. In the UK, for example, the Bank of England (the national bank of the UK) began to conduct research into cryptocurrencies, which they summarized in a report. Even more recently, Venezuela started to experiment with the idea of creating their own cryptocurrency to overcome economic problems and international embargos against them.

CHAPTER 4: #HASHGRAPH -

WHO? WHAT AND WHY?

Changes haven't stopped happening. We are still seeing new technology arising offering new alternatives to just about everything. And in the world of cryptocurrency, though relatively young, one of those new innovations is Hashgraph, the logical evolution of blockchain technology.

WHO ARE THEY?

Hashgraph is one of the newest kids on the 'block' in the cryptocurrency community and, as is often claimed by its creators, it may lead to the end of blockchain and to a new kind of decentralized platform, which they believe will be Hashgraph itself. Hashgraph is the creation of Swirlds, a company that provides support to developers to build applications that rapidly achieve distributed consensus. In computer science, a distributed consensus is where all parts of a system come to an agreement on information within itself, specifically in regards to transactions and events, and the data within them. If all information is agreed upon, then a distributed consensus has been reached. If there is conflicting information then there is a problem, perhaps with faulty parts of the system, and it may not function correctly or at all. Distributed consensus plays an important role in how cryptocurrency works, especially so with blockchain. This is because, apart from being an issue with the system, it can also prevent fraudulent transactions.

Swirlds was co-founded by Leemond Baird (CTO), and Mance Harmon (CEO) both of whom hold over 20 years of experience in their chosen fields and have paved the way for a number of startup companies before coming together to found Swirlds and develop Hashgraph.

Before founding Swirlds, Leemond Baird was a professor of Computer Science in the United States Air Force Academy, a senior scientist, and co-founded numerous startup companies. He also holds a PhD in Computer science. As CTO, Leemond is the driving force behind the innovation of Swirlds and holds a key interest in math, particularly in how it can be used to create new algorithms and create a distributed consensus. He is also credited as being the inventor of Hashgraph and has been very active in educating the public about it.

Mance Harmon is also incredibly experienced, having formerly worked in numerous international companies and startups, and US government agencies. He also previously founded a number of high-tech startup companies, worked as a program manager for the missile defense agency and also worked on cybersecurity at the United States Air Force Academy (the same institution Leemond had previously worked at). Mance also was the Head of Architecture and Labs at Ping Identity, a partner company to Swirlds, and holds an MS in Computer Science.

Hashgraph is one of their latest and most ambitious projects, which has placed them in the spot-light. In some senses, it is a culmination of all their work.

WHAT'S SO SPECIAL ABOUT HASHGRAPH?

Hashgraph has a variety features that make it distinctively different from blockchain. Here are its biggest features summarized:

- Fairness - Hashgraph is able to process transactions as they happen, it does not rely on miners.
- Speed - Hashgraph is believed to handle as much as 250,000 transactions per second, perhaps in even more.
- Security - Events are shared randomly and cannot be stopped, manipulated or ordered by someone else.
- Scaling - Hashgraph does not have issues with scaling and may well be able to continue growing infinitely.

HOW HASHGRAPH WORKS

Hashgraph has some major similarities to blockchain-based technology as it is a platform used to build applications on. It is also completely peer-to-peer with no central server, but its differences are significant enough to recognize it as a new type of information sharing technology. Hashgraph operates a 'gossip about gossip' protocol.

This is similar to the gossip protocol used by the blockchain for Bitcoin, but with some major differences - most importantly, miners are not encouraged to mine blocks based on the reward fee they will earn. This is because the gossip about gossip protocol does not need this process at all, instead information is gossiped by one computer (or 'node') sharing all its information with another at random. This information includes all the information of every transaction it knows that the other doesn't already know. The latter node takes on board this information and randomly shares it with another, and the process continues like this and eventually updates the entire Hashgraph, rendering a transaction complete.

As Leemond Baird puts it "Everybody talks to everybody all the time." This process is an example of what distributed consensus is, Swirlds' area of expertise.

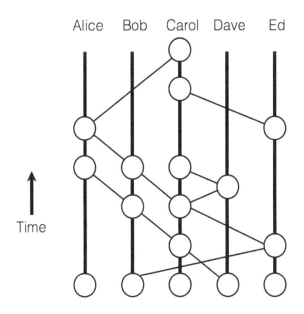

Commonly shared image showing what a Hashgraph is. We can also see how it got its name - it's a graph that contains hashes.

On the above diagram, we can see how information is shared within a Hashgraph. The vertical lines represent an individual node while the circles represent an event, which is when two nodes share something with each other. You can see leading off from them are lines from other nodes which shows you who was involved in the transaction - or the parents of the event. These events are not necessarily financial transactions. They can sometimes just be the act of sharing information, usually of other transactions that have been made within the Hashgraph around the same time. As time goes by and more transactions are made, the Hashgraph gets longer.

Theories of such platforms, often referred to as voting algorithms, have existed before, but there has been less interest in producing it as there are issues with bandwidth. This is because in such an algorithm if information needs to be accepted by all nodes in the system, it will take a very long time, longer than with other algorithms, as all information theoretically needs to be shared, compared and then agreed upon. However, with the gossip about gossip protocol, Swirlds have found a way to overcome the issue of bandwidth by adding the element of randomness. By having nodes share all the information they have with another node chosen completely at random, all information is spread much fast throughout the network. There is no comparing or waiting to share information.

This technique allows the Hashgraph to process transactions at an incredibly fast rate, with some sources claiming a capacity of up to 250,000 transactions per second, possibly more, a speed which is almost unheard of in the cryptocurrency community. This is partly down to how lightweight the system is.

Though the Bitcoin blockchain is also quite light at only 60 GB, the Hashgraph is a tiny 1 GB. It is so small some have even raised the possibility of using phones as nodes (a possibility discussed further in *Chapter 6: #Conclusion - What's Next?* section *There are some big challenges still to come*).

Hashgraph's speed is so quick it not only puts other cryptocurrencies to shame. It's an embarrassment to most of the world's largest and most technologically advanced banks, too (another reason for them to be afraid). Such a transaction speed would mean people would no longer need to wait days or even until the end of a week until their transactions, both in and out, are processed. By adopting Hashgraph, people will always be sure that their balance is correct and this can also lead to a reduction of accidental double spending.

Hashgraph's speed is also related how it is divided into rounds of voting, another crucial part of how Hashgraph works. Though, it should be mentioned that Hashgraph's voting algorithm works without the voting, which is often called virtual voting. This can be done by focusing largely on the first events created by each individual in the first round, which are referred to as witnesses, voting on their presence in the second round and confirming them in the third round (meaning they have now been fully processed and completed). The reason this is done is because these are the events that require the most computing power and by focusing on these events the speed of the Hashgraph remains high and computing costs remain low. Events that follow the first initial event created by a node do not require so much computing power as they are usually just sharing information among each other. Once all the individuals involved in a Hashgraph have shared their information that was first added to the Hashgraph in their first event, a new round can begin.

In the second round, when the voting takes place, at least three thirds need to vote that they can see an event for it to be accepted, but if there is a tie, then they will also vote yes. If it is accepted, it is largely referred to as 'famous.' By separating the events into rounds, it becomes harder for attackers to influence the system or make malicious transactions. A correct consensus is always reached and once it has been reached, it cannot be changed. This is because these rounds of voting continue and as they do, all information is collected eventually.

If, somehow, an attacker manages to pass numerous rounds, by the tenth round there is a Coin Round. Again, the events vote for a supermajority or tie and anyone who gets it simply votes yes. But if you do not collect a supermajority or a tie, they will vote randomly based on the numbers in their digital signature. However, it should be pointed out that this is extremely difficult to get to this point. The attacker would have to be extremely powerful, to the point of possibly controlling the majority of the Internet. More can be read about Hashgraph's security in *Chapter 4: #Hashgraph vs. Bitcoin: Why Hashgraph Wins.*

Hashgraph is also a lot fairer than blockchain technology as transactions go through almost exactly as they are made because they do not depend on when miners will mine the block created that their transaction is included in. In a sense it is even more decentralized than blockchain, with no individuals or groups with the power to influence the system. Though events can be time stamped by their creators, all events are accepted by the calculated medium time all witnesses became aware of it, which makes it fairer by relying on the system not on a third-party, such as a miner.

On top of that, because of the way Hashgraph works, it does not need proof of work or proof of stake for individuals to make transactions. People simply create events whenever they like.

A commonly shared picture used to show the difference between blockchain and Hashgraph.

On the left is blockchain, which is depicted as a log with a few cut off stubs at various points. On the right is Hashgraph, a tree that is woven together. It depicts how with blockchain technology all information leads to a dead end, while Hashgraph is completely interconnected, all information is shared.

It should also be mentioned that Hashgraph is not related to Hashcoin. Hashgraph are yet to release a coin yet as they are still in the development stage of the technology and are yet to release a cryptocurrency. Due to the similarity in names, it is likely that when Hashgraph has a coin ready its name will be very different, probably not related to Hashgraph (more on this in *Chapter 6:*

#Conclusion - What's Next? section *A coin is needed*).

Despite not being ready to provide cryptocurrency transactions yet, if people are interested in developing applications on Hashgraph, they are able to get a license from Swirlds to do so which will provide them with an SDK (Software Development Kit). However, such individuals need to bear in mind that at the time of this ebook being published, it is not completely open-source. Those that are interested in doing so should have some knowledge of Java, the coding language used for Hashgraph. They would probably also benefit from first downloading a demo version of Hashgraph to develop a better understanding of how it works. It even includes a demo app that runs the algorithm and shows you how the Hashgraph grows.

Hashgraph also has potential in a variety of other ways. One of those ways is gaming and may be able to host server-less online gaming. Such a development could really speed up waiting times and also provide a fairer gaming environment.

Other possible uses include recording the ownership of property, whether that's music, land or stocks for example. After the transaction has been made, it can easily be dug up when needed.

CHAPTER 5: #HASHGRAPH VS. BITCOIN - WHY HASHGRAPH WINS

Bitcoin's blockchain started interest in cryptocurrency, but as a concept was never finished. Hashgraph improved on many issues faced by blockchain and brings new ideas to the table. It is the next step in cryptocurrency.

WITHOUT BLOCKCHAIN AND BITCOIN THERE WOULD NOT BE HASHGRAPH... BUT...

There is no doubt that blockchain and Bitcoin were amazing inventions. Those that have worked on them and continue to work on them have contributed to a new world change.

Without that change it is very possible Hashgraph would never have existed, it started the conversation about what cryptocurrency should be. However, it has become obvious that it has some key flaws that are not likely to be fixed anytime soon.

Some of these major flaws include:

- A slowly diminishing rate of money creation - as time goes by it gets harder to create new Bitcoin.
- Limited amount of Bitcoin - only 21 million Bitcoins can ever be created.
- Reliance on miners - miners can choose which transactions to include in blocks.
- Complicated programing language.
- Lack of leadership.

BITCOIN HAS BECOME AN INVESTORS' TOY

The prices of bitcoin are insane and a very big problem. Bitcoin has become an investors' toy with them pumping a lot of money into it. So much money, in fact, that the price continues to shoot up at an unbelievable rate which simply cannot last and will burst leaving many with huge possible losses. In March 2010, one Bitcoin cost approximately $0.003, and now in 2018, eight years later, one Bitcoin cost $7640.01 (at the time of writing this book). A lot of the time when there is news on cryptocurrency, it's about Bitcoin and it's almost constantly rising prices. And a lot of the time it's promoted as a good thing, particularly in financial circles, who often promote it as something you need to get involved in urgently - the next big thing! But they could not be more wrong.

So why is this so bad, you're asking? Well, it's because Bitcoin was designed so that coins could be created at an increasingly slow rate. Already approximately more than half of all coins have already come into existence, and by the mid-2020s, the growth rate will almost be nothing, with some critics saying that it will basically become a fixed supply of money. This has also lead to immense competitiveness amongst miners as there are now more of them than ever and they are fighting over a slowly shrinking supply of Bitcoin.

Being an investor's play-thing also leads to many other issues aside from massive potential losses. Firstly, its unsustainable nature will make it impractical to use in everyday life, specifically for employers when paying their employees - the prices of products would need to change too frequently along with pay packages. To counter this issue, supply and demand must be met, but it is very unlikely that any such kind of design feature will ever be implemented. Secondly, further to the first point, there is no regulation of Bitcoin. No one decides how it develops and grows and how it should be used - this is dictated by the market, miners and investors, all of whom answer to no specific entity. Because of this, it is very unlikely that any kind of regulations will ever be put into place to ensure stability and implement a strategy in case of economic collapse. Can you see any of the groups mentioned above taking responsibility for a financial crash? Bitcoin has no real voice to stop it being manipulated and no one has real enough power to challenge unfairness.

Thirdly, large scale investment in Bitcoin has made investing in the currency now unaffordable to much of the general public, which means it's becoming harder for them to get involved and it will not lead to a shift in wealth. In fact, it may even lead to the exact opposite. There are already people who are Bitcoin millionaires, meaning that if Bitcoin became an international way to make transactions tomorrow, for example, the new people entering this system would have an extremely unfair disadvantage.

On top of this, people who are only investing in Bitcoin to make a profit are not spending their Bitcoin. They are only keeping it to speculate on its inevitable price rise. They are not interested in seeing Bitcoin become a way to pay for services, for example. This has led to a system where the people who were involved in the early conception of Bitcoin and the speculators that followed, are they only ones who are rewarded by it. Those that actually use it to operate in the economy by conducting business deals, for example, are not rewarded, giving them little incentive to bother using it. The same can be said about the majority of blockchain-based cryptocurrency that relies on miners.

Hashgraph may be able to overcome many of these issues. By being a patented technology, Swirlds could possibly be able to implement more control over how it is used. If so, they will be able to monitor and regulate the system to ensure it grows at a healthy rate, preventing severe drops or rises that can lead to an economic crisis. It could also be possible for Swirlds to invest in creating a full-time team that works solely on monitoring such events and to ensure the system is operating safely and legally. Further to that, if Hashgraph gained governmental support, it may be possible to put laws in place in regards to how people invest in any cryptocurrency used on a Hashgraph. This would probably be the best direction to move in because unless governments feel like they can trust cryptocurrency, they will never adopt it.

But perhaps one of the biggest reasons Hashgraph will triumph over the currently domineering Bitcoin is that Bitcoin has not been built to last, while Hashgraph does not have any potential future issues.

SECURITY

Security is the number one priority for many who are involved in cryptocurrency - investors, transaction makers, and miners alike. Without a stable and secure network to operate on, cryptocurrency is pointless. Not many people will move to a system less secure than the current system. Most people cannot afford to risk losing their earnings. This is an issue with Bitcoin and other blockchain-based cryptocurrencies and is perhaps one of the biggest reasons more people are not willing to get involved yet.

There have been a number of attacks on those who purchase Bitcoin in the last few years and the exchange companies you can purchase it from. At this point we should quickly explain what a virtual wallet is (for those unaware). A virtual wallet is a place where money - cryptocurrency or physical currency - is kept to perform online transactions. Generally speaking, you should be very vigilant with your cryptocurrency and keep is safe and secure in your virtual wallet on your computer - this is usually the safest place for it. Alternatively, if you own a vast amount of cryptocurrency, it is advised that you keep in what is known as 'cold storage', which usually takes the form of an external hard drive or even a USB stick.

However, in order to get cryptocurrency into your nice and safe wallet, if not by mining or if it was not gifted, you need to purchase it via an exchange company. Usually these companies offer a variety of cryptocurrencies in exchange for physical currency, such as the US Dollar. Once your money has been exchanged for cryptocurrency, you need to withdraw it from the exchange and place it in your virtual wallet. It is very important that you do this quickly after the exchange has taken place because leaving your cryptocurrency in an exchange is a very reckless thing to do as they are incredibly well-known for getting attacked. It's actually the number one way people lose their cryptocurrency.

Some of these attacks have been huge, for example, in 2016 in Hong Kong, 119,756 Bitcoins (approximately $78 million) were stolen from users from a company called Bitfinex. However, before that in 2014 Mt. Gox, formerly the world's largest Bitcoin exchange, lost $500 million worth of Bitcoin from 24,000 of its customers. To make things worse, due to the lack of legal expertise in the area and lack of laws and policies, it is very likely its customers will ever see this money again. This is only part of the story. Many others have also lost huge amounts from similar attacks.

All these attacks have not helped the image of Bitcoin and cryptocurrencies in general. Those against the idea of cryptocurrencies, such as banks and governments, to suggest that the industry hasn't changed since the early dark days when criminals used it, have also used such incidents.

Hashgraph is largely safer than blockchain-based cryptocurrencies due to the gossip about gossip protocol it uses. As all information is shared all the time at random it is the most decentralized system ever devised. This is a major plus in regards to security because in order to hijack a Hashgraph you would need to attack a large portion of all the individuals involved in it at the same time. With Hashgraph to attack so many people at once is almost impossible. In comparison to leader-based or centralized systems, for example, if the leader is removed the system falls apart.

Attacking one individual has very limited effect with Hashgraph. For example, you cannot attack one individual node to prevent a transaction occurring. Once a transaction has been made, it is immediately gossiped. Though the node is no longer participating in the Hashgraph after it has been taken out, the information is still spread to all the other nodes and the transaction is validated after a consensus has been reached. This is called ACID (Atomicity, Consistency, Isolation,

Durability) compliant. It can ensure transactions are valid even if an error occurs, such as a power failure.

The randomness of Hashgraph makes it safer in other ways too. It can also prevent malicious transactions from happening, such as someone trying to purchase something that has already been purchased by another. Because information on a Hashgraph is gossiped to all participants, whoever made the transaction first will ultimately win as not only will it reach consensus quicker, it will also be clearly visible to anyone who checks the history of the Hashgraph. This prevents anyone from getting in the way of your transaction. Such individuals would not even be able to get help from others within the Hashgraph to carry out this deed. This is called Byzantine Fault Tolerance (or BFT).

Byzantine Fault Tolerance (BFT)

This refers to a particular characteristic of blockchains, particularly its ability to tolerate what is called "byzantine failures." The level of such tolerance is crucial for blockchains with respect to its ability to keep its records reliable, transparent, and hack or tamper-proof.

Now you may be wondering why the term "Byzantine"? Well, it's because BFT embodies a resolution to what's referred to as the "Byzantine generals' problem, which is a logic-related predicament that was first described in an academic paper that was published by researchers Marshall Pease, Robert Shostak, and Leslie Ramport in 1982.

To get a better picture, think of a group of Byzantine generals with their multitudes of soldiers circling around the castle of an enemy and getting ready to lay siege of that castle. All of the armies commanded by each of the generals must simultaneously attack the castle in order to successfully capture the castle. But they have one major concern: the generals know that there's a turncoat within entire army's ranks. And so they face the problem or challenge of being able to successfully conquer the castle despite having an anonymous traitor in their ranks.

You can think of this problem as one that is also faced by numerous computer networks. When an army or a group attempts to decide collectively on their next courses of action, there is a chance that certain members of the group may send a different messages or information as to what to do next. Basically, it means that there's a chance that these rogue members may give information on the group's next course of action to some members while giving contradictory information to other members. When this happens, the army may encounter challenges in terms of effectively coordinating its actions. When there's division due to confusion wrought by the rogue members giving contradictory information to different members of the group or army, it'll be impossible for the group to act as one, i.e. in unison. This can lead to defeat in battle. In other words, united they may stand but divided they will fall.

The illustration I gave can be used to describe many of the problems faced by many computer networks. You may think of a distributed computing environment, i.e., a computer network, as an army or group of soldiers that need to collectively act in unison in order to win their battles. A computer network is one with numerous users, programs, servers and types of nodes. You can also think of this as a blockchain.

Because the individual users, programs, servers, nodes and computer that comprise the network need to act in unison in order to function correctly, the risk of breaking down due to unreliable or rogue members or actors who act differently from the rest of the network. If some servers aren't able to consistently pass data to the other servers in the network, it can lead to a server cluster's breakdown. In short, a computer network may fail or collapse if all of its members fail to agree on a single networking protocol for relaying or trading information.

To ensure reliability, computer networks have to be set up or constructed in such a way that they're able to address the Byzantine generals' problem of the risk of traitors screwing up their military operations through what's called as Byzantine Fault Tolerance or BFT, the importance of which is utmost in blockchains. Why is the BFT of such importance in a blockchain?

Traditional computer networking environments run through a centralized database or a governing authority that manages networks and executes corrective actions in the event of erroneous or fraudulent transactions. But blockchains are anything but traditional in the sense that they don't have any central authorities or databases - they're decentralized. Blockchains are only able to ensure legitimate transactions via the networks' or communities' consensuses, which makes blockchains very powerful.

And this type of reliance on consensus among the network members makes Byzantine faults, i.e., occurrence of Byzantine general-types of problems, a very serious issue for blockchains. This is because, unlike traditional networks, where central authorities have the authority to correct or cancel erroneous or fraudulent transactions, blockchains have none. So if one member of a network provides inconsistent or even contradictory information to other members of that network, the reliability of that network is ruined with no recourse for restoration or correction. That's why unless blockchains can absolutely trust everybody in the network to be honest or accurate, they'll need to find solutions for the occurrence of Byzantine faults or problems that may occur as a result of rogue members proliferating malicious, misleading, or inaccurate information on transactions.

Unfortunately (or fortunately for Hashgraph), there's no single best remedy for Byzantine fault tolerance or BFT within blockchains. Many of the most powerful and popular blockchain systems have so far relied on the PoW or Proof Of Work system to ensure legitimacy of transactions. As you already know, this method requires a group of people called miners to solve very laborious and complex mathematical problems or algorithms to authenticate transactions and add them to the blockchain. In Bitcoin's situation, the proof of work is created through what's called a "hashing algorithm", which usually takes a relatively long time to complete.

Under the PoW system, transactions can't be added into the blockchain unless the party that's responsible for adding the data invests a substantial amount of time on the data. This requirement is a very practical way of minimizing risks for manipulation. Why? It's because in order to manipulate or undermine a network's consensus, that person or party with the malicious intent will need to put in so much time just to substantially influence a blockchain. Time that can be put to more productive use. And in very large blockchains such as Bitcoin's PoW takes a substantial amount of time to create and in the process, gives BFT to the blockchain.

However effective PoW is when it comes to giving high BFT to a relatively large blockchain such as Bitcoin's, it has a significant tradeoff: it needs to exert a very huge amount of computational effort only for the purpose of ensuring fault tolerance. This means only the most powerful computers will do, which also means huge electricity or power costs. A possible solution to this, which may not need as much computing power, is to rely on node voting as well as majority consensus for fleshing out byzantine faults. But this alternative has its concern too, and that is it will only work in terms of protecting against Byzantine faults if an overwhelming majority of a network's nodes act with legitimacy on a consistent and continuous basis. But if the number of rogue users or nodes in the blockchain get close to 50%, consensus on the legitimacy of transactions may become vague.

While the concept of the BFT can sound so highfaluting that it seems to only be a concern to people who create cryptocurrencies, which to a great extent is true, it may not always be the case. But because blockchain technology still continues to evolve in many different places, understanding BFT may also be of utmost importance to people who don't work with cryptocurrencies. In particular, BFT may also be of importance to those who are looking to use the concept of blockchains as some sort of practical solutions to their non-cryptocurrency related challenges. And in particular, what can work for others in terms of providing BFT may not necessarily work for all. Take the case of using PoW, which works for Bitcoin, and an entity that doesn't involve cryptocurrencies, say a health care provider.

For Bitcoin, PoW is crucial for BFT purposes. But if a healthcare provider is required to use a huge amount of computer resources just to hash data in order to create proofs of work, it would be very inefficient on the part of the healthcare provider due to the different nature of its business and operations. Reliance on node votes may be the more sensible approach for BFT for a healthcare provider.

Why is this so? It's because of the participants in a healthcare provider's data network. The people who participate in a healthcare provider's computer network are those who provide their real identities and are altruistic. Bitcoin's network on the other hand, is unregulated and very anonymous, for which node voting is significantly riskier than a PoW method for solving Byzantine faults. And while BFT may have worked well for blockchains such that of Bitcoin's, there's a very good chance that it won't work as well for future blockchain applications.

BFT, in computer science is a system's ability to maintain consensus, meaning all parts of the system agree on all the information that has been shared. If a system is unable to keep a consensus, then it has a low BFT, and systems like this can be manipulated by attackers. A high BFT ensures security and the Hashgraph algorithm has an extraordinary high BFT. Though, it is possible to cheat the system by creating two events at the same time, what is sometimes called double spending, however, mathematically it has been proven that this doesn't matter, because eventually consensus must be reached and only one event can be legitimate. This is largely down to how it can be divided into rounds. As mentioned in the previous chapter. This can be done by focusing largely on the first events made by each individual voting on what events they can see from the previous round. Once all the individuals involved in a Hashgraph have shared their information that was added to the Hashgraph in their first event, a new round can begin, and so on.

It is possible for attackers to try and cheat the system by creating two events at the same time in the same round. But because the witnesses will always vote on the events they can see, the duplicated event will always be discovered and not accepted within the supermajority. If there is conflicting information, eventually on the tenth round there will be a Coin Round, as explained in *Chapter 4: #Hashgraph - Who? What and Why?*

With such a decentralized and secure system in place the Hashgraph might not just be safer to use than blockchain, but all other current systems used to make transactions with FIAT currencies. If this is true, it really can be a viable option for those who are concerned about the security of cryptocurrency.

Hashgraph being a patented technology also offers additional protection. Legally speaking, anyone who attempts to put a fork in the system and divide it into two platforms with a slightly different trajectory, like with Ethereum and Ethereum Classic, would not have any legal rights to continue operating that platform and it would eventually be shut down. This is very important because cryptocurrencies need to be safe, there is no point to simply create a new cryptocurrency all the time after an attack. One eventually needs to win and take over as the standard for transactions to be made.

While there are many strengths to the Hashgraph's security, Swirlds still needs to find a better way for people to exchange currency to remove itself from the image problem Bitcoin suffers from. It may be good to have a more fortified platform to make transactions on, but it won't be worth much if people are not able to keep it safe when it is not in their virtual wallets. Nevertheless, it is an issue for the future once Hashgraph has launched their own cryptocurrency.

HASHGRAPH WINS

Hashgraph in so many ways looks not just a like a better alternative, but like the most logical evolution from the blockchain and Bitcoin. This is largely down to how Hashgraph has managed to find the best way to operate a voting algorithm by implementing intelligent and secure distribution consensus theories. Before voting algorithms were previous viewed as too slow due to lack of bandwidth and therefore not practical.

The Hashgraph voting algorithm has many major advantages over the two other algorithms used largely used for blockchain-based technology - PoS (Proof of Stake) and PoW (Proof of Work). With the PoS algorithm, funds are locked up and need to be voted for to become a block and enter the blockchain, however, if someone enters a malicious block, funds can be lost. Blockchains based on PoS also distribute access of blocks to miners by the amount they own. For example, if someone owns 5% of a specific cryptocurrency, they will then also have access to 5% of all the available blocks in the system. This system was designed to overcome issues of cryptocurrency devaluing over time if people sell it in favor of FIAT currencies.

PoW also has some major flaws. While it is highly regarded as perhaps one of the safest ways to operate cryptocurrency, it relies on miners a lot which has led to a number of problems. The process can take a long time for a transaction to be completed as newly created blocks first need to be found miners, then blocks need to be mined and all other nodes need to be made aware of the new block in the system to accept it. On top of that transactions need to wait for others to be completed, slowing the process down even further. However, the biggest problem with PoW is that miners decide when transactions will take place based on the fees they will receive from mining the newly created block. So, even before the mining can begin, miners will decide or not if they would like to include you in their block. If you your transaction it to take place soon then you need to pay more. While this is unfair to those that do not have the funds to pay large mining fees, you also need to consider the position the miner is in. Just to mine one block requires a lot of computing power and because of that, a lot of electricity. Some estimates suggesting as much as 1.57 US households per day of electricity can be used for a single block to be complete. This is obviously very expensive and the miners need to cover their bills.

Hashgraph is the best way to overcome all of the issues mentioned above for both PoS and PoW blockchains. It guarantees fairness by being able to handle all transactions in the same way without relying on miners or any other factors. With Hashgraph, all transactions are processed at the time they are made. This is because by relying on distributed consensus, mathematically all information will be shared, making the process fair. On top of that, with Hashgraph all information is shared for all transactions, including who was involved in a transaction, what was transacted and when it happened. With PoS and PoW, some of this information can be hidden. This means that Hashgraph guarantees even more fairness by ensuring all information is logged with all details, meaning people cannot hide anything fraudulent. It also triumphs over leader-based networks too, as in such an algorithm, the leader has complete control and can decide the order in which transactions are made.

When looking at Bitcoin and its blockchain specifically, there are a number of flaws that need to be addressed. Starting from the very beginning, it should be mentioned that Bitcoin was developed as a prototype for cryptocurrency, it was never completed by Nakamoto before they disappeared. People have referred to the writing style used by Nakamoto in Bitcoin's white paper. It is clear from his writing style that they were very intelligent, but it also comes across as an experiment. There are numerous other areas that also show the creation of Bitcoin was clearly an experiment, such as the coding language used for Bitcoin, C++. While C++ is still used for a variety of purposes, it is a difficult language to learn to use and is not as popular as it once was. JavaScript for example, which was adopted by Ethereum, is easier to use and is a language known by a lot more people, meaning it is more open for new people to get involved with. The same is also true with Java, another more logical language, which is used by Hashgraph.

The key thing to remember about Bitcoin being a prototype is that prototypes generally do not work on their first attempt, or at least some functions may not work as initially desired. Often with a prototype, unforeseen problems arise that need to be taken into consideration. After recognizing and correcting them a better version can be released, but there has never been a Bitcoin 0.2, and now too much has been invested in Bitcoin for anyone to ever consider shutting it down and starting again.

However, it should be mentioned that some parts of Bitcoin's source code have been modified significantly and it is possible for those involved with Bitcoin's development to add new changes to an extent. Though, there are some parts of Bitcoin that they will never be able to change. Some of the things that cannot be changed include the basic structure of the system, most importantly, how blocks are created and mined. Possibly Hashgraph's greatest benefit is removing the need for blocks to be mined. An important question to ask is: can blockchain-based technology really claim to be decentralized if it needs miners to complete all transactions? In a sense, miners are the replacement of bankers in the new cryptocurrency world. Giving miners the choice of which blocks to mine creates an unfair system.

Hashgraph has the advantage of coming along later after Bitcoin and the variety of other cryptocurrencies that followed. Swirlds, while in the process of developing the Hashgraph are able to observe and learn from the mistakes that were made with Bitcoin its blockchain. With strong leadership at its helm and an experienced team, Hashgraph has a clear direction to follow and the ability to strategize effectively when they come across the unforeseen. It is not likely to end up with the same flaws.

CHAPTER 6: #HASHGRAPH VS.

THE REST OF THE WORLD

Any cryptocurrency built on top of Hashgraph not only has to beat Bitcoin, it has to beat all the other blockchain-based cryptocurrencies. Then it needs to show the political and financial world that it is not only the best option but the safest and most logical.

THE OTHER CRYPTOCURRENCIES

Aside from Bitcoin, Hashgraph still has competition from the other less well-known cryptocurrencies. Though many boast the unique qualities that they think will allow them to take over the industry, Hashgraph's speed and security are likely to make it the world's choice. Perhaps the greatest thing to remember when comparing blockchain-based cryptocurrency with whatever cryptocurrency will be built on top of Hashgraph, is that they are on entirely different platforms. Blockchain-based cryptocurrencies are most based on Bitcoin, attempting to improve its flaws, while Hashgraph is trying to improve the deeper flaws concerned with blockchain - hence why Hashgraph's inventors often claim it is the end of blockchain.

SECURITY... AGAIN

As mentioned before in the previous chapter, security is a major concern for many involved in cryptocurrencies.

Some of the major attacks on other cryptocurrencies have caused a lot of concern and have led some to make possibly poor decisions. Once such incident was when Ethereum was attacked and up to $55 million was believed to have been stolen. This all happened because a hacker came across a critical flaw in Ethereum, specifically multi-signature wallet. To return the stolen Ether, Vitalik and his team forked the blockchain, creating two different Ethereum blockchains - one where the attacker kept the stolen Ether, another where the system was reset a whole day and the stolen Ether was not taken. The idea was that people would stop using the former older system and start using the new one. However, that didn't go to plan and a number of people continued to use it. Many of which did so because in the older version their transactions that took place that day were still valid, but not in the new system. They named the alternative older version of Ethereum Classic and it is now being developed by a whole new team independent of the original.

Many have been critical of the decision made by Vitalik and his team. Creating another version of Ethereum was probably not the wisest decision and goes against the main point of developing cryptocurrency - to create a decentralized and world unifying way to make transactions. By splitting the community, Ethereum stepped further away from reaching that point. Cryptocurrencies need to be better prepared to respond to such problems. As mentioned before, the creators of Hashgraph at Swirlds have the experience and wisdom not to make such errors and are most likely able to implement a better strategy to stop it happening.

WORLD GOVERNMENTS

One of the biggest barriers cryptocurrencies need to overcome is the approval of world governments. But it should be said that not all countries are on the same page when it comes to cryptocurrencies. While some countries are researching cryptocurrencies and blockchain technology, seeing how they could be used, often the loudest voices in the political world are against accepting them. Some of blockchain's staunchest opponents are the EU's Central Bank, which is strongly supporting the idea of blocking it, mainland China where it is already banned, and Russia, among a number of other nations. One of the main reasons is stability, citing the lack of control over Bitcoin. Though, as mentioned before, this is largely down to Bitcoin being an investor's toy, however, Ethereum and other popular cryptocurrencies can also be viewed in this light as well.

World governments also have no control over the creation of new coins too, as they do with their own physical currency, which they can print when necessary. And on top of it all, many are also afraid that if the world were to unite under one currency, this would have negative effects on poorer nations where prices may rise exponentially.

A further issue is the lack of knowledge of cryptocurrency in the political world. Many politicians are just not interested and don't have much of an opinion on the topic. This is a problem that can be seen whenever technological changes start affecting politics - politicians usually do not recognize their significance. It's an issue that has also been raised recently in regards to AI and other new technologies as well.

However, Hashgraph is patented, which means it is legally protected on a number of levels. Having a legal backing will also help it gain the respect of world governments and banks as it is playing by their rules to a certain degree. Instead of completely turning their backs on governments and banks, like Bitcoin and other cryptocurrencies appeared to at the beginning, Hashgraph may be able to bridge the gap between them. If possible, this may be able to accommodate a smoother transition to a cashless cryptocurrency world. This is probably the best path Hashgraph's success. But it will still involve many years of talks and negotiations between Swirlds and governments, and if accepted by the international community, will probably involve some kind of treaty on its use.

EXPERIENCE AND LEADERSHIP

Leemond Baird and Mance Harmon are perhaps two of the most experienced individuals working in cryptocurrency, both with 20 years of experience in computer science and both hold degrees in the area. Vitalik Buterin, the founder of Ethereum, is only 24 years old (at the time this book was written). Though there is no doubt he is a genius, like many others that have created their own cryptocurrency, it is likely that his young age and inexperience led him to unwise decisions, such as the one discussed in the previous section. Not only do the leaders of Swirlds have a better understanding of the technology involved, they also have solid leadership and direction. On top of that, they are an established company with numerous employees to count on.

But perhaps the most important thing they have is a solid understanding of the importance of a consensus algorithm and by applying it to cryptocurrency have managed to bypass many of the issues blockchain-based cryptocurrencies had.

HASHGRAPH WINS AGAIN

Hashgraph, again, triumphs over its alternatives. This is largely down to the same reasons it triumphs over Bitcoin - speed, security, fairness and removing the need for miners. Most cryptocurrencies are just trying to improve on Bitcoin. Hashgraph is trying to improve on blockchain.

If we look at history, whenever a new invention comes along, immediately after you usually find a number of people fighting to create the best possible version. The car is a good example of this. Invented in 1886 by Karl Benz, numerous different interpretations soon followed with different ideas on how different parts of the car should operate, such as the gearbox. It wasn't until 20-30 years later when a universal system was put in place and considered standard. Though this took place more than 100 years ago and, of course, there are numerous manufacturers of cars, the way they operate is largely the same. There are also examples of this happening in the 21st century too. Like operating systems used for phones. Today Android is the most used operating system, defeating most of its rivals with only Apple and Microsoft offering any real alternative.

We're seeing this again with cryptocurrency and eventually, one will overpower the rest and become dominant. Generally speaking, it's the one that's easier for everyone to use and Hashgraph doesn't require its users to be very technically minded to use it.

CHAPTER 7: #CONCLUSION -

WHAT'S NEXT?

If you're still skeptical about the practical superiority of Hashgraph over the blockchain, consider that more and more well-known companies have tied up with Swirlds in order to use Hashgraph in their operations. Four of these companies include VMS Software, Inc., OpenCrowd, MZ, and Mingo.

VMS SOFTWARE, INC. (VSI)

In January 2018, Swirlds and VSI formally agreed that VSI would use the Hashgraph technology to allow its customers to securely and swiftly operate and implement new generation network distributed applications. And VSI's customers aren't ordinary individuals and companies, mind you. Their clients include multinational institutions that rely heavily on mission-critical systems - companies like transportation companies, governments, power plants, manufacturing companies, international retailers, stock exchanges, and multinational banks. The reason why many such companies trust VMS is because the OpenVMS operating system is considered to be one of the most secure operating systems in the world today. And for them to choose to use the Hashgraph technology says a lot about the superiority of Hashgraph!

So what makes VSI's OpenVMS operating system so reliable? For one, the uptime and stability levels of this operating system remains to be the industry's gold standard. It's that good that its stability and uptime isn't measured in weeks or months but in years. That's right - years! And by incorporating the Hashgraph technology into their system, VSI's customers will have the capability to operate and implement new generation network distributed applications that have both unparalleled speed and security.

According to the CEO of VSI, Duane Harris, they had evaluated numerous blockchain technologies for several years already but they have been challenged to find one that can provide both the security, scalability, and ease of use that their very discerning clients need. The applications that their clients run process tens of thousands of transactions every second, which means they require speed without sacrificing security and scalability. Harris said that of all the alternative they've evaluated, only Swirlds' Hashgraph was able to provide the answer to their and their clients' needs and that VSI is excited to lead the way when it comes to innovating operating systems by working together with Swirlds.

OPENCROWD

OpenCrowd is a top-notch technology and design firm that provides companies the world over - from established ones to startups - with customized blockchain business solutions. You can thus consider OpenCrowd to be a blockchain specialization company that has helped hundreds of businesses make their new business models a reality and speed up the progress of new and purpose-driven apps through the application of emerging or next-generation technologies. The kinds of smart applications they create for clients are those that optimize machine learning, analytics, and blockchain technologies. The company main clients are investment banks that concentrate on providing clients real time access to markets, collateral management, and settlement services. They also cater to young start-up companies that in the fintech, intellectual capital, government, and healthcare sectors.

OpenCrowd is a company that truly believes many emerging technological innovations in the future will be founded on machine learning-powered and decentralized applications. And for that OpenCrowd has incorporated new blockchain technology platforms for its applications, and one of them is Hashgraph.

On 25 January 2018, OpenCrowd and Swirlds announced that they were partnering together to create new decentralized applications. This is one of the ways that modern, cutting-edge companies adapt to the rapidly evolving markets that rely on distributed ledger technology for optimal scale, trust, security, and overall performance. In particular, Swirlds and OpenCrowd have joined forces to further improve the functions and features of the Hashgraph platform. The 2 companies will work together to create the best and most advanced applications that utilize the distributed ledger technology for their customers. For OpenCrowd, this is an opportunity to further advance its application development and give its customers unparalleled security and performance at lower costs. OpenCrowd's CEO Sushil Prabhu said that partnering with Swirlds to use provide top quality Hashgraph-based solutions to their clients at unmatched speeds will help the OpenCrowd to expand its market and provide its corporate clients with innovative distributed ledger applications that can meet their trust, throughput, and critical scale needs.

MZ AND MINGO

Two other notable enterprises have joined the ranks of Hashgraph supporters and users: MZ and Mingo. MZ is one of the world's biggest games and applications development companies and is the company behind one of the most played mobile games in the world, Game of War. It will start using the Hedera Hashgraph platform and it believes that through said platform, it can create new games and applications whose speeds are beyond imagination that will translate into totally new gaming experiences.

Mingo is a cryptocurrency-oriented application, which has been working on providing a service that will allow its users to access and use all of their social media messenger accounts with just one very secure app. Mingo users will be able to link conversations and contacts across different messaging apps.

Mingo also utilizes the same structure to facilitate payments for services and products via their own Mingo Plugin Economy. For this, the company is heavily reliant on micropayments, which the Hedera Hashgraph platform is well-suited for. Mingo is looking forward to the Hashgraph platform's ability to make their facilitation of payments ultra-fast and secure.

A COIN IS NEEDED

Firstly, it should be said that Hashgraph not related to Hashcoin (sometimes spelled HashCoin)! The Hashcoin is an Estonian cryptocurrency that belongs to a completely different system that is not related to the Hashgraph. As exciting as Hashgraph is, the platform is yet to launch a coin that can be traded. This is because Swirlds are still yet to release the Hashgraph to the entire world yet as it is still being worked on. Before any cryptocurrency can even be thought about, the Hashgraph must be finished.

It should also be considered that there may be a possibility for more than one Hashgraph to exist and within each Hashgraph there may be more than one cryptocurrency supported. A coin or coins may be released by different companies as applications built on top of a Hashgraph or numerous Hashgraphs, perhaps as part of a partnership with Swirlds. In this sense, Swirlds may retain control of the Hashgraph or multiple Hashgraphs to keep them secure while different companies run their applications on top. The reason this may happen is that Swirlds specialization is distributed consensus and their knowledge of finance may be limited. So, they may just stick to creating and maintaining the Hashgraph (or Hashgraphs) and leave the cryptocurrency on top to financial professionals.

This may have both positive and negative side effects. By separating the financial side from the technical side, a better functioning cryptocurrency could be produced where individuals are actually in control of their own areas of expertise. It should be mentioned that not all individuals involved in cryptocurrency have knowledge of finance, many specialize solely in computer science. However, the negative part of this development could be that there is less control by separating the growth of the Hashgraph from the possible cryptocurrencies that are created on top of it.

The issue around Hashgraph being a patented technology also affects what cryptocurrencies may be built on top of it. If Hashgraph became an open-source technology, it would be easier for people not related to Swirlds to get involved and create their own cryptocurrencies on the platform. But if it remains not open-source, it will likely be a company that will buy rights to operate the Hashgraph algorithm or Swirlds themselves. However, it should be remembered that just because Swirlds have patented the Hashgraph now, does not mean they will keep it that way forever. After a certain point, they remove the patent once the Hashgraph is clearly secure and credible. But then the question emerges; how will Swirlds benefit from this? Only time will tell.

Other things to be considered are what will the Initial Coin Offering (or ICO) be? An ICO is when investors are offered a new cryptocurrency in exchange for another. It may be possible that there might be a grand release which can be used to gain publicity. Whatever the occasion maybe, actions should be taken to ensure any Hashgraph-based cryptocurrency doesn't become an investors' toy the same way

Bitcoin has, and it is able to continue growing the money supply at a stable rate.

THE HEDERA HASHGRAPH PLATFORM

Leemon Baird and Mance Harmon didn't just put up Swirlds, they also created the Hedera Hashgraph Platform. It's a company that's separate and distinct from Swirlds, and is focused on creating distributed public ledgers utilizing the Hashgraph algorithm. In short, Hedera is Swirlds' sister company that will leverage on Swilds' Hashgraph patented technology.

Hedera Hashgraph - as a startup company and platform - will concentrate on 3 key services: cryptocurrency for facilitating micro transactions, distributed ledger for micro storage, and smart contracts. And while these services aren't exactly new ones considering these are already provided by existing blockchain platforms in the market, what makes Hedera's versions of these services is the promised speeds at which it promises to render these services. By blending these 3 services, Hedera Hashgraph will make it easy to create apps with the Hashgraph technology. And because the Hedera Hashgraph platform also provides vigorous API support, the platform will help developers create Hashgraph-based apps more easily.

And speaking of cryptocurrencies, Hedera plan to launch theirs by the second half of 2018. The startup has been able to raise close to $20 million in funds from a wide range of accredited investors that include the Digital Currency Group, which is a cryptocurrency holding company. This planned launch is one of the biggest things that the investing-minded members of the Hashgraph community have been waiting for with much excitement and the announcement of such a plan has made many of them jump in the air and pump their fists with a loud "yeah!" accompanying them.

This is very exciting news indeed because of the current limitations of the biggest existing cryptocurrencies, which include Bitcoin and Ethereum. To be more specific, the 2 cryptocurrencies' turtle-like pace of processing transactions and their relatively high transactions costs are two of the biggest hindrances to them being accepted in the mainstream as a legit alternative mode of payment. Think of it this way: would you be willing to wait upwards of 10 minutes for your transactions to settle? I don't think so. But this is the average speeds at which transactions involving Bitcoin and Ethereum are processed and authenticated. Now you know why despite all the hype about these major cryptocurrencies, they remain to be nothing more than an off-market payment mode and a vehicle for financial speculation.

The brains behind the Hedera Hashgraph function know that they can process a very high volume of transactions way faster than the existing blockchain technologies of these 2 major cryptocurrencies and do so at a much lower cost! One basis for this strong belief is that Bitcoin and Ether's software processes transactions linearly, i.e., as a string or chain of transactions, compared to the Hashgraph platform that can process transactions in a parallel or simultaneous fashion. This means the platform will be able to effectively support micropayments and transactions.

And not only that, the Hedera Hashgraph platform will also be able to support smart contracts. This means contracts will automatically be executed or cancelled upon the completion or non-completion of specific requirements, respectively.

The Hedera Hashgraph platform utilizes a mathematical approach called DAG or Directed Acyclic Graph. But it's not only Hashgraph that utilize this type of data structure. Cryptocurrency platforms IOTA and Byteball does so too. Unfortunately, researchers have found a couple of security issues with the IOTA platform and these have resulted in updates to the platform's software. Ever since, some of the researchers' claims were challenged by IOTA.

Fortunately for Hashgraph, it takes a different approach to consensus or finalizing transactions compared to IOTA. According to Mance Harmon, the Hedera Hashgraph platform has been able to accomplish what is called an asynchronous BFT or Byzantine Fault Tolerance, which is a security feature that allows a computer network to still function properly even if rogue members of that network attempt to undermine the consensus by maliciously spreading wrong information to other members of the network. Because of this, Hashgraph may be considered as the industry's gold standard!

Interestingly, the Hedera Hashgraph cryptocurrency, which has still yet to be named, is technically not a cryptocurrency but a token. What's the difference? In a nutshell, coins (cryptocurrencies) have their own separate blockchains while tokens operate on top of an already existing blockchain that helps makes it possible to create decentralized applications, such as the Hedera Hashgraph platform. But eschewing the technicalities, the Hedera Hashgraph tokens are available for purchase via its presale but this unlike Bitcoin and other altcoins that are available to everybody regardless where in the world they live. The Hashgraph tokens are only available for United States accredited investors.

Users of the platform and its developers will receive Hashgraph tokens in exchange for their participation on the platform. And by virtue of the token's restricted circulation, access to the tokens will be kept private for the duration of the platform's startup phase and as of the moment, all signs point to the possibility that no open sale will be conducted for the token. Instead, tokens will only be available to big contributors and investors to the Hedera Hashgraph platform whose identities are verifiable. It's probably meant to protect the token from speculators and potentially malicious members that can make the tokens price as volatile and unstable as most cryptocurrencies'.

The platform also approaches corporate oversight from a rather unique perspective, something that blockchains of cryptocurrencies don't do. The platform - according to Mance Harmon - has formed a global governing council that is comprised of 39 global blue-chip companies that come from a diverse range of industries, which includes Swirlds. Each member of the governing council will be given a 2.6% share of the company and they will help guide the startup company in making very important decisions. As a governing body, the council chooses members of the startup company's Board of Directors as well as the sub-committees that will be responsible for managing the platform's key operational aspects. Harmon believes that through such a governing council, the platform will be able to achieve a level of mainstream acceptance and legitimacy that existing cryptocurrency platforms are unable to.

Unlike majority of the current blockchain-based projects in the world today, the Hashgraph algorithm is patented under a specific developer, which is Swirlds. For the privilege of using the Hashgraph algorithm, Hedera will pay Swirlds 10% of the revenues it will earn.

Lastly, the Hedera Hashgraph platform is very different than blockchain-based cryptocurrencies in terms of regulatory compliance. While cryptocurrency platforms do not require compliance with anti-money laundering and KYC (know your customer) laws and regulations, the Hedera Hashgraph platform will make room for applications that comply with anti-money laundering and KYC regulations. Also, the platform will also feature an opt-in escrow facility that can make it possible to link real identities to cryptocurrency wallets, if circumstances warrant it. These features clearly show that the platform can't be used by criminals and money launderers for any of their financial shenanigans.

If you're looking to invest in a token that has the potential to grow in value over time through steady and legit gains and not through mere wild speculation, then the yet to be named token that Hedera Hashgraph will roll out in the latter part of 2018 can be a potentially good investment for you. However, you have to make sure that you're a United States accredited investor. Otherwise, you won't be able to invest in this soon to be released token. And even if you're an accredited investor in the United States but you're looking for a highly speculative investment, this isn't the kind of investment you're looking for. The key features of the platform, and consequently the token, are such that speculation and wild price swings are highly unlikely.

THERE ARE SOME BIG CHALLENGES

STILL TO COME

Hashgraph is still in the process of being developed and just like anything that has not yet been released to the general public, it needs to gain a following to have a successful launch. To reach that point, Hashgraph needs a community to grow around it. This community is needed to spread the word by explaining how Hashgraph works and engage with outsiders, as well as bring new ideas to the table. A strong community also has the added benefit of being able to help or start industries that can work with or around Hashgraph too, such as trading. This is in the process of happening and provocative statements such as Hashgraph being the end of blockchain have garnered a lot of attention. But this is still the beginning and a lot more work needs to be done, most likely after or as a coin is released and people are able to make transactions. However, they still have been active. A quick Google search will show you that Swirlds have been very busy promoting Hashgraph, particularly Leemond, releasing videos on YouTube explaining the technology and also releasing the White Paper for Hashgraph back in 2016.

It should be mentioned though, that some cryptocurrency experts are concerned because Hashgraph is a patented technology. This concerns them because it means it is not open-source like many of the other well-known blockchain-based cryptocurrencies. This has created a negative image of Hashgraph in the eyes of few cryptocurrency enthusiasts who do not trust anything that is not open-source. To them it looks like it just a tool for industry, such as those that handle finance and banking. Many cryptocurrency users got involved to get away from these institutions. Their point of view is that if it is not completely decentralized Swirlds may have selfish ulterior motives and, therefore, are no different from central banks. However, being patented does offer a lot of protection of the technology and ensures Swirlds are the only company that can develop it. In fact, part of the reasoning why the technology is not open-source is because Swirlds are still are not finished with it yet, and they want to ensure the technology is successful before releasing it to the general public. This is just in case faults can be found and to ensure success ensure success. But it doesn't help the image. Swirlds needs to find a way to overcome this potential image problem, to divert attention away from it and, when asked why it is patented, provide logical and fair answers. Hashgraph needs to win over cryptocurrency enthusiasts to create a strong community.

Though, it has also been announced that Swirlds are working on releasing an open-source version later, which gives hope to some that maybe it is not a tool for industry and it really might be a useful alternative to blockchain. However, bear in mind the possibility that the open-source release of Hashgraph may coincide with a cryptocurrency being launched or another kind of application built on top of it.

Many of the bigger issues Hashgraph will face are issues any successful cryptocurrency will face as it gains momentum and strives to be the universal way transactions are made. One of those issues is what to do if people do not stop using old cryptocurrencies? It is likely there will be a fair degree of resistance from those that have invested money in alternative cryptocurrencies and they obviously do not want to lose that investment. This is a problem because if there are numerous cryptocurrencies available in the world, these people will not be able to properly trade with each other. It would actually be easier for them to trade using FIAT currencies, which completely defeats the point of cryptocurrency in the first place. It is supposed to unite the world, not divide it any further. With the world united under one cryptocurrency, anyone will be able to do business with anyone they like wherever they may be. There needs to be a hospitable way to solve this problem and encourage other cryptocurrency users to divest and move to Hashgraph when it is ready.

Another big problem that not just Hashgraph faces, but all cryptocurrency in general, is that there are a lot of people in the world that do not have Internet access or even access to a computer. Cryptocurrency only being available in the developed world is not enough and not fair. In such places making the shift from physical cash to cryptocurrency will be incredibly difficult. But we also need to ask ourselves whose responsibility is this? Industry or world governments? Sadly, it looks like world governments will not lead the way on this one as they are often very slow to react to technological change and not likely to come to an international agreement.

However, we are seeing some progress on this issue. For example, in India, between 2014 and 2016, the number of Internet users leaped from approximately 233,152,478 to 462,124,989. India has almost doubled its Internet users in the space of two years by investing in providing better infrastructure, a trend that is likely to continue in the next few years to come. But it should be mentioned that a large number of these new Internet users do not own a laptop or computer but are actually cellphone users. This is because cellphones are much cheaper and available often on contract with a service provider. This is also true in China as well where the number of cellphone users outranks other devices. To overcome this issue, it is likely we will see an increase in smartphone apps, specifically virtual wallets that can transfer cryptocurrency. To ensure Swilds does not miss out on these huge markets, it needs to make sure it understands this and be prepared to invest in it.

Further to this issue, the problem of Internet access may be solved in the near future. We are already seeing possible solutions from both

Google and Facebook, among others, who are trying to find ways to provide the entire Earth with Wi-Fi either by high altitude balloons or drones. But then it should be considered what effect will Hashgraph-based cryptocurrency have on market economies? How will people buy simple things like fruit from a market stall? With their phones?

Until we live in a world where transactions can be made around the world with one (or possibly multiple) cryptocurrency without restrictions the dream is not complete. Though a lot of innovation has taken place in the last 10 or so years, we may not see the full benefits of it globally for another 20 or 30 years.

MANY POSSIBILITIES

If Hashgraph turns out to be a success it may well provide the shake-up capitalism needs to revive itself and birth a new and fairer system. We may see new wealth creation on a global scale that could lead to a world where wealth is more evenly shared, and quality of life improves. The professions people specialize in may drastically change, with more investing their education in IT. If Hashgraph becomes an international currency and replaces all other currencies around the world, this could also lead to better diplomacy between nations and more multinational companies, with people being able to work and live where they like. Some of these things are already in the works, such as the growing trend for employees to prefer to work from home and experiments with universal income in places such as Finland. Hashgraph could even up being the driving-force these things need to take full swing.

We also should not forget there are other uses of Hashgraph aside from cryptocurrency. It could also be used for a variety of other purposes where sharing of information is needed efficiently and securely. Even if the technology that Swirlds has developed is not used, the theories and methods devised by Leemond Baird and co, will likely have a legacy and effect future related technology.

The simple answer to the question "What will the world be like if Hashgraph is a success?" is that no one knows. As with all change in society, whether that be social, technological or political, those that are responsible for implementing them never fully grasp how their change will affect people as there are always changes that weren't anticipated. Changes may solve one problem but can sometimes lead to new problems or just reshape the old problem into another more complicated one.

There are numerous examples of such changes in technology in recent times that had unforeseen effects. Perhaps one of the best-known examples is Facebook. The social media platform Facebook was never expected to have such a big effect on people's lives. For many, it has become an addictive habit, their main source of news, and it is possible that it has been manipulated and used as a tool for sharing fake news. And, if we look at social media in a more general light, it was designed as something to connect people, but it now looks like it may have the opposite effect. In some respects, it pushes people further apart from each other, especially strangers, the exact opposite of its desired purpose.

Similar things have happened with other technology, too. Even Bitcoin fits into this definition - designed as a better way to process transactions, it is largely now seen as a tool to invest in. It is almost impossible for inventors to predict the effect their technology will have on the general public.

One thing is for sure though, a real solid change is needed before the economic world falls apart. Blockchain technology, while an amazing invention, was never going to last as there were too many issues with speed, security and scaling among others, mostly originating from the fact that the technology was never finished. The problems with blockchain are only going to get bigger as it becomes more popular. On the other hand, Hashgraph looks like it has a real potential to make a big change in the economic world or at least act as a catalyst of change in various areas and ease the world's entrance to a new form of capitalism, whether it will be named post-capitalism or something else.

REFERENCES:

1. https://blockgeeks.com/guides/proof-of-work-vs-proof-of-stake/

2. https://www.nasdaq.com/article/byzantine-fault-tolerance-the-key-for-blockchains-cm810058

3. https://www.cryptoninjas.net/2018/02/10/vms-software-partners-swirlds-hashgraph-build-distributed-applications/

4. https://ph.linkedin.com/company/opencrowd

5. https://www.prnewswire.com/news-releases/opencrowd-and-swirlds-the-hashgraph-company-partner-to-enable-development-of-next-generation-decentralized-applications-300588335.html

6. https://www.forbes.com/sites/jeffkauflin/2018/03/13/hedera-hashgraph-

thinks-it-can-one-up-bitcoin-and-

ethereum-with-faster-transactions/	-

73d64a20abcb

7. https://www.investinblockchain.com/

hedera-hashgraph-platform/

ABOUT THE AUTHOR

Mario Robertson is a Marine Corps Veteran, who studied Health Care Management at Park University. Upon completion of his bachelor's degree he produces non-fiction informational books, as well as volunteers his services at the local VA. Mario is also a licensed insurance agent who serviced over 35 states during his time as a broker. He currently resides with his wife, and 2 children in the great state of Kansas.

OTHER BOOKS BY (MARIO ROBERTSON)

AirBnB: A Beginning Users Guide

Inner Peace: The inconvenient Truth

Thanks for Reading!

Make sure you get a copy of the books mentioned above.

I would be so grateful if you please leave me a review . I would love to get your feedback.

www.ingramcontent.com/pod-product-compliance
Lightning Source LLC
Chambersburg PA
CBHW051055050326
40690CB00006B/723